THEO

prepares for Christmas

All the children are so excited. It's the last day of term. The Christmas holidays have begun "Mummy, look at my art folder!" says Theo.

Theo, Baby Paul and Mummy go to the bakery where Daddy works. "My Daddy bakes the best bread in the world!" thinks Theo as he watches him take a tasty cob from the oven.

When they get home Theo has a bath while Mummy
changes Baby Paul's nappy. Just then Daddy arrives
back from work. "Hello Daddy," shouts Theo,
splashing about in the water.

It's time to eat. Theo is laying the table while Daddy cooks and watches television at the same time. "Don't burn the supper, Daddy," says Theo. "I'm starving!"

"Shh! Don't wake the baby,"
says Mummy.
"I can't wait until tomorrow.
I've packed my bag already,"
Theo tells her.
"I hope Daddy's team will win
the match."

The start of a new day. Everyone is busy. Theo doesn't need any help this morning. There's so much to be done before they leave.

"You can have a ride on the donkey when we get there," Theo tells Baby Paul.
Meanwhile Mummy and Daddy struggle to fit all the luggage in the car.

More luggage! It's a good thing Theo and Baby Paul don't take up too much room. Aunty Rose is coming as well.

While Mummy is doing some last minute shopping, Theo has a little word with Father Christmas.

Let's go! At last they're on their way.
Theo holds Baby Paul on his lap. It's a
tight squeeze. Teddy has to travel on the
roof rack.

"It's good to stretch your legs," says Aunty Rose. Theo gives Grandma a big hug. It's lovely to see her again.

Grandma takes Theo and his cousins along to choose the Christmas tree, while she buys the turkey.
"Do you think this tree is tall enough?" asks Clara. Luis doesn't care. He's only interested in the ducks.

Theo and Pedro are jumping up and down with
excitement.
"That turkey looks delicious" says Grandad, and
Daddy calls out "Cheers Everyone! Merry
Christmas!"

THEO DISCOVERS THE WORLD

Dear Parents,

These delightful stories, with their charming illustrations, are intended for you to enjoy with your child.

Set aside a quiet time to share the book and give yourselves the pleasure of each other's company. Use the illustrations as a stimulus for conversation, as a starting point for your imagination. Allow your child to discover the satisfaction of reading as communication.

The text is deliberately kept short, but acts as a springboard for discussion between you. With the very young this may go no further than looking at the lively illustrations and identifying objects, colours and situations. With older children it may also include concepts of their own relationships, emotions, behaviour. Respond to any comments, answer any questions and talk about what is or might be happening in each picture.

Theo lives in Spain and children are children all over the world. Take this opportunity to explore differences and similarities between people and cultures at home and abroad. The guidelines below are a few suggestions of topics that might come up for discusssion on each page.

Let the child take you by the hand and lead you through the book.

Jana Pattenden

Last day of term. What do you feel like at the end of term? Do you sometimes make presents for Mummy and Daddy at school? What do you like to do during your holidays? Does Theo live in a village or a town? How are children going home from school? Talk about the dangers of the traffic on the roads. Do any of the children look like your friends? Who looks as though they work hard? Who looks mischevious?

Bathtime. What is Theo doing in the bath? Do you like having a bath? Why isn't Baby Paul having a bath with Theo? Do you think he is safe on the changing table? Why is the radio on the seat of the toilet? Is it plugged in? Why have the suitcases been packed? Who can you see in the photograph on the wall? Where has Theo's Daddy been? What will he do?

In the kitchen. Does Theo know how to lay the table? Can you lay the table? What is everyone going to sit on? What is Daddy cooking? What is he looking at? What is Mummy doing? What can you see in her fishing net? Why is Baby Paul quite contented? Is he going to eat too?

The bakery. How is bread made? What is an oven, and how does it work? Is the baker's oven the same as the one in your kitchen? What kind of bread and pastries can you recognise? Which man is Theo's Daddy? Do you think he is the owner of the bakery? What time do bakers start work in the morning? Why is Baby Paul crying? Where is Theo's Mummy going? What is Theo doing? What is he saying to his Daddy? What is his Mummy saying?

Bedtime. Who are the people in the living room? Why are there so many people? What are they talking about? What are they watching? Do you think their team is going to win? Why is Mummy telling Theo to keep quiet? Is he going to go straight to sleep? What is Mummy going to do when Theo has settled down? Is she going to watch television or will she finish the packing? What is she knitting?